New

Practical English I

contents

Unit 01

Food and Eating Out

1. What Do You Want to Eat?

Max : Sally! What are you going to eat for dinner?

Sally : I'm going to eat some meat and vegetables.
And what do you want to eat?

Max : I want some fried rice.

Sally : Sounds good. Where are we going?

Max : I want to go downtown to a Korean restaurant.

Sally : Well. I know a famous Korean restaurant in downtown.

Max : Great! Let's try it.

Sally : Sure. Let's leave now. I'm starving.

Max : OK. I'll get ready really quick.

2. How Would You Like Your Beef?

Waitress : Are you ready to order now?
Jason : Yes. I'll have some salad and beef, please.

Waitress : How would you like your beef? Rare, medium, or well-done?
Jason : Well-done, please.

Waitress : Sure. Anything to drink?
Jason : Do you have coffee or tea?

Waitress : Yes, we have both. Which one would you like, coffee or tea?
Jason : I'd like coffee.

Waitress : How would you like your coffee?
Jason : No sugar, please.

Waitress : Thank you, sir. I will get it ready.

3. What Would You Like to Order?

Waiter : What would you like to order?
Sandy : I'd like ham and eggs, please.

Waiter : How do you want your eggs?
Sandy : What are my choices?

Waiter : Scrambled, sunny side-up, over-easy, and over-hard.
Sandy : I'd like sunny side-up, please.

Waiter : Is there anything else?
Sandy : A glass of orange juice, please.

Waiter : What size would you like?
Sandy : Make it small, please.

Waiter : Thank you. I will be back in a minute.

4. I'd Like to Reserve a Table for Dinner.

Receptionist : Kookje Restaurant. How may I help you?
Customer : Yes. I'd like to reserve a table for dinner.

Receptionist : How many people are you expecting?
Customer : Six people all together.

Receptionist : Would you like to reserve a large table?
Customer : That sounds good.

Receptionist : All right. May I have your name, sir?
Customer : My name is Jimmy Carson. C-A-R-S-O-N.

Receptionist : What time will you be arriving?
Customer : Around 7:00 pm. tomorrow evening.

Receptionist : All right, Mr. Carson.
We have reserved a large table at 7:00 pm. tomorrow.
Thanks for calling, Mr. Carson.
Customer : Thank you very much.

Receptionist : You're welcome, sir.

5. I'd Like to Reserve a Table for Dinner.

Sandra : Max! Let's eat out, shall we?

Max : I'm sorry. I'm broke.
I've already gone through my paycheck for the week.

Sandra : Don't worry about it. It's my treat.

Max : Are you sure? You're so kind! Thank you.

Sandra : You're welcome.

Max : So, where are we going to?

Sandra : Well. I want to eat noodle or rice.
What about the Chinese restaurant near our school?

Max : That's a good place.
The food in the restaurant is delicious and cheap.

Sandra : I agree. And they are kind, too.

Max : Let's go there right now.

Sandra : Sure.

Review Exercises [Unit 1]

Read the sentence and write an appropriate answer.

1. What are you going to eat for dinner?

____

2. And what do you want to eat?

____

3. Where are we going to?

____

4. Are you ready to order now?

____

5. How would you like your beef? Rare, medium, or well-done?

____

6. How would you like your coffee?

____

7. What would you like to order?

____

8. What size would you like?

____

9. How many people are you expecting?

____

10. May I have your name, sir?

____

Storytelling (1)

Nationality

Excuse me, everyone. Listen to me, please. We can look over them. First, we can look at the man in the yellow shirt with a white tie. That's Mr. George Eliot from New York. He's American. Next to George, we can see two people. They may be a couple. She has short hair. She has really beautiful hair. Her name is Emily and his name is Harry. They are from England. Next, we can see the tall man standing on the exit. The man is Mark from Toronto, Canada. The girl after him is Sandra who lives in Deli, India. Her friend is Yuko who lives in Tokyo. They will meet their French friend, Lurie. The man wearing a traditional dress is Mohamed from Saudi Arabia. The people talking to each other are Dolley and Nick. They say they are from Canberra, Australia. We can see the last person in a long dress. The passport says that she is Yuna Lee who lives in Hong-Kong.

Fill the information in the vacant box.

Name	Country	Nationality
George	America	American
Emily and Harry	England	
Mark	Canada	

Grammar Exercises [1]

1. The woman makes _____ by selling clothes.

① enough moneys　② a lot of moncy
③ many moneys　④ much moneys

2. Many people have been _____ work for a long time.

① for　② from
③ to　④ out of

3. She can't buy any shoes because they are out of ___ .

① amount　② store
③ shop　④ stock

4. I think 20 _____ is not a cheap price in this store.

① finance　② cash
③ dollars　④ currency

5. The plant is good for economic and _____ areas.

① medical　② medicine
③ medication　④ medically

6. The students are both sick; _____ is at school today.

① either ② neither
③ both ④ each

7. _____ of the adults is attending special night classes.

① One ② Few
③ Little ④ Some

8. He will be here by that time if he is _____ on earth.

① live ② alive
③ lived ④ lively

9. In this country, _____ people live there.

① much ② many
③ a little ④ little

10. Would you like _____ hot coffee?

① any ② little
③ some ④ few

Task Tips

Ingredients for Food

2 cups heavy whipping cream

2 teaspoons salt

2 teaspoons ground black pepper

1/2 teaspoons crushed red pepper flakes

1 teaspoon ground white pepper

1 cup chopped green onions

1 cup chopped parsley

1/2 pound shrimp

1/2 cup shredded Swiss cheese

1/2 cup grated Parmesan cheese

1 pound dry pasta

(Sauce : http://allrecipes.com/Recipe/Cajun-Seafood-Pasta/Detail.aspx)

Unit 02

Health and Care

1. I'm on a Diet.

Jimmy : Would you like to have some ice-cream?
I've got a variety of flavors for you to choose.
Sara : What kinds of ice-cream do you have?

Jimmy : I have strawberry, peach, chocolate, coffee, and vanilla.
Sara : Wow! Great! I wish I could, but I can't. I'm on a diet now.

Jimmy : Come on. Please have a bite.
Sara : I'd better not.

Jimmy : Gee! You are really strong-willed.
Sara : I'm sorry. I can't eat sweet thing for the time being.

Jimmy : Well, I'd better not tempt you.
Sara : Thanks for your understanding.

2. The Tooth Is Killing Me.

Mary : Hi, Charles! What happened? Your face looks swollen.
Charles : I went to a dentist.

Mary : What's the problem?
Charles : I got a cavity filled today.

Mary : Oh, that's too bad. Did it hurt?
Charles : I don't even want to talk about it. It killed me!
I can't stand the pain.

Mary : Well, I guess you're in pain.
You should take care of your teeth.
Charles : Yes, I will brush my teeth.
How many times should I brush them?

Mary : You'd better brush them three times a day.
Charles : Yes, I will. I should do it.

3. Now I Have a Terrible Headache.

Susan : Ken! You look so tired.
Didn't you get enough sleep last night?

Ken : No. I met some of my friends last night.
And we had a party until late.

Susan : I see. So, you look so bad!

Ken : Now I have a terrible headache, and my head is spinning.

Susan : I think you need to go home and take a rest.

Ken : You are right. But I can't go home alone. I am so tired.

Susan : Don't worry. I'll give you a ride home.
But next time, don't have a long party, OK?

4. You Have a Strong Stomach.

Sara : What's wrong? You look so worried!
Bob : I have a stomachache.
I think I got some bad food at lunch today.

Sara : Oh, really? That's too bad, but we ate at the same place.
Bob : Yes, we sure did.

Sara : By the way, I don't have any problem with my stomach.
Bob : You have an iron stomach. But my stomach isn't so strong.

Sara : So what should you do now?
Bob : I will go to a clinic. I must hurry up.

5. You'd Better See a Doctor First.

Harry : I feel awful this morning!

Olive : You don't look so good. What's wrong?

Harry : I've got a runny nose.
I have a headache, and I'm aching all over.

Olive : That's too bad. What are you taking?

Harry : Nothing so far. Do you have anything I can take?

Olive : Let me see. In the meantime, drink lots of hot water.

Harry : Oh, I see. You give me a good suggestion.

Olive : And I think you'd better take a rest for the time being.

Harry : No, I have some classes in the afternoon.

Olive : You'd better see a doctor first.

Harry : Yes, I will make an appointment at a clinic.

Review Exercises [Unit 2]

Read the sentence and write an appropriate answer.

1. What kinds of ice-cream do you have?

____

2. Oh, that's too bad. Did it hurt?

____

3. How many times should I brush them?

____

4. Didn't you get enough sleep last night?

____

5. I think you need to go home and take a rest.

____

6. You don't look so good. What's wrong?

____

7. That's too bad. What are you taking?

____

8. Do you have anything I can take?

____

9. I think you'd better take a rest for a time being.

____

10. You'd better see a doctor first.

____

Storytelling (2)

Introducing the House

I will show you this house. It was built ten years ago. That is, it was built in 2010, and there are a lot of space in the house.

You can go through the front door into the hall. On the left is the bathroom and the livingroom. They are quite spacious. From the livingroom window, you can see a nice view of the park and street. Next to the livingroom, there's a kitchen. The door is at the end of the hall. The kitchen is not quite big, so we can always enjoy eating in the livingroom. There are four bedrooms. Two room are nice and big, and the other two are small. I show you bathroom. The bathroom is on the corner of the hall, and it is on the left side of the livingroom. The bathroom is between the bedroom and the kitchen.

Read the passages above and write the rooms in the picture.

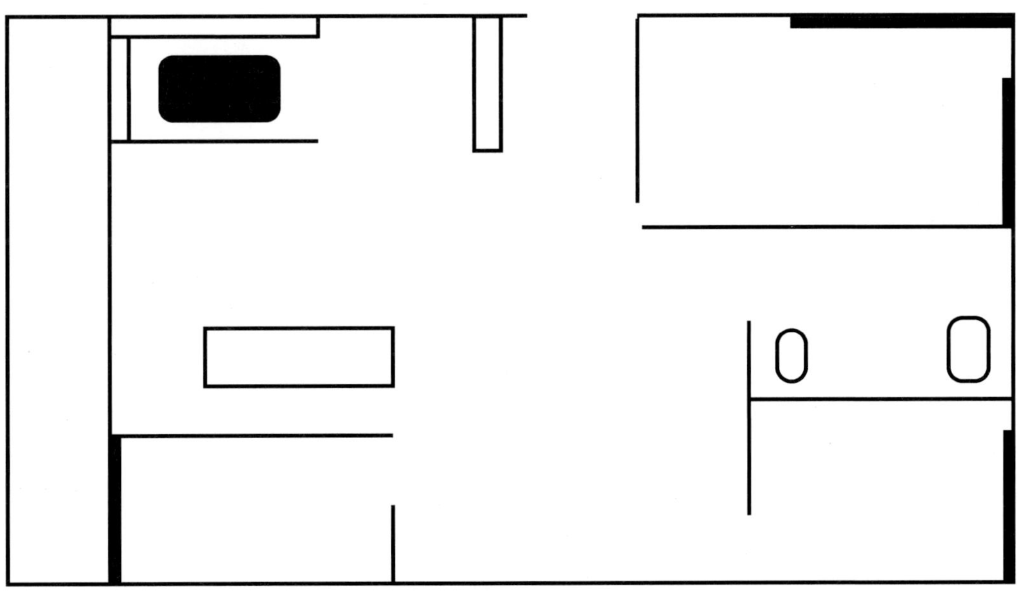

Review Exercises [2]

1. The family owns a _____ car with leather seat.
   ① thirty year old ② thirty years old
   ③ thirty year olds ④ thirty years olds

2. I think that the prices are just too _____ .
   ① expensive
   ② dear
   ③ high
   ④ exalted

3. The bank manager has _____ confidence in his work.
   ① some ② many
   ③ few ④ a few

4. The only way to help _____ is to find ways to help themselves.
   ① poor ② a poor
   ③ the poor ④ poverty

5. _____ friends are leaving the country for the future.
   ① The your best ② Your two best
   ③ Best your two ④ Your best the

6. She talked so _____ that they could not write down it.

① fast ② rapid

③ quick ④ swift

7. You are going _____ fast. Please slow down.

① too much ② very much

③ much too ④ much

8. He has _____ studied it for a long time.

① yet ② already

③ still ④ no

9. She _____ comes to work by subway.

① at the times ② from time

③ sometime ④ nearly always

10. I know that I won't win the game _____ .

① in the long run ② still

③ however ④ already

Task Tips

국제 음성 기호(2005년 기준)
닿소리표

	양순음	순치음	치음	치조음	치조후음	권설음	경구개음	연구개음	구개수음	인두음	후두개음	성문음
비음	m	ɱ		n		ɳ	ɲ	ŋ	ɴ			
파열음	p b	ȹ ȸ		t d		ʈ ɖ	c ɟ	k ɡ	q ɢ		ʡ	ʔ
마찰음	ɸ β	f v	θ ð	s z	ʃ ʒ	ʂ ʐ	ç ʝ	x ɣ	χ ʁ	ħ ʕ	ʜ ʢ	h ɦ
접근음		ʋ		ɹ		ɻ	j	ɰ				
전동음	ʙ			r					ʀ		я	
탄음		ⱱ		ɾ		ɽ						
설측 마찰음				ɬ ɮ		ꞎ	𝼆	ʟ̝̊				
설측 접근음				l		ɭ	ʎ	ʟ				
설측 탄음				ɺ		ɭ̆						

한 칸에 두 개의 기호가 있을 경우, 왼쪽이 무성음이고 오른쪽이 유성음이다. 단 반기식음 ɦ는 예외이다. 어둡게 칠해진 칸은 조음이 불가능하다고 여겨지는 칸이다. 회색기호는 국제음 기호의 비공식 확장이다.

Unit 03

Housing and Facilities

1. Do You Have Air-conditioning in Your Office?

George : It's very hot today.
Kitty : Yes, it sure is. It's terrible weather.

George : Do you have air-conditioning in your office? It's sweating here.
Kitty : Well, there's air-conditioning in this room.
Do you see the air-conditioner there?

George : There is an air-conditioner on the corder.
By the way, it is still hot here.
Kitty : The problem is that the air-conditioner is not powerful enough.

George : I guess it sure is. You should repair it, I think.
Kitty : Well. You are right. Anyway, let's move to the other room.
The room has central air-conditioning.

George : That's a good idea. Let's go to the room right away.

2. The Bathtub Is Clogged up Again.

Monica : Hello, is Jimmy there?
Jimmy : This is he speaking.

Monica : Hello, Jimmy. This is the tenant of the Kookje Apartment. My room number is 213. I have some problems in my room.
Jimmy : What problems do you have?

Monica : I guess my kitchen sink is clogged up again, and so is the bathtub.
Jimmy : All right, I'll send someone over tomorrow.

Monica : I really appreciate it. But I want you to send someone to fix it today. It's really a bother. I can't cook. And I can't take a shower.
Jimmy : Oh, that's terrible, I'll be up in a few minutes.

Monica : Thanks. I appreciate it.

3. The Drain Has Gone Wrong in the Room?

Brian : What's wrong with the drain in your room?
Olive : It's clogged and the water won't go down.

Brian : Let me take a look. It's clogged with hair.
The water won't go down.
Olive : Well, I guess the people didn't clean the bathtub.

Brian : You're right.
Olive : But what should I do now?

Brian : Don't worry. I've got some acid here. It'll dissolve the hair down.
Olive : Oh! It works well. Good job.

Brian : Now you'll have to clean your bathtub every time after you use it.

4. My Water Faucet Is Dripping.

Ester : Oh, no! The water faucet is dripping badly again!
Brian : You're going to have a big problem.

Ester : Yes. I must get it fixed as soon as possible.
Brian : Don't you want to get it fixed now?

Ester : I wish I could, but I can't now.
Brian : Why? What's wrong?

Ester : I must go out now. I have an appointment in thirty minutes.
Brian : Well, if you need anything, just let me know.

Ester : Oh, can you give me a ride? My car is still in the shop.
Brian : Yes, I can help you. You are having bad luck these days.

5. I Have an Apartment Available?

Bob : Hello. I'm calling about the apartment you advertised.
Manager : Yes. What kind of apartment are you interested in?

Bob : I'm interested in a one-bedroom. Do you have one available?
Manager : Yes. I have one. When do you need it?

Bob : Maybe next week. What can you tell me about this apartment?
Manager : Well, it's a one-bedroom apartment.
The monthly rent is $600, with a $300 security deposit.
Gas and water is included. You pay electricity only.
Both the heat and stove are gas.
You have a parking space at no extra charge.

Bob : Sounds good. May I come over tomorrow to take a look?
Manager : Sure. What time would you like to come?

Bob : How about 3 PM.?
Manager : Good. May I have your name, please?

Bob : My name is Bob Harrison.
Manager : Mr. Bob Harrison. I'll see you tomorrow afternoon.

Review Exercises [Unit 3]

Read the sentence and write an appropriate answer.

1. Do you have air-conditioning in your office?

____

2. Hello, is Jimmy there?

____

3. Oh, no! The water faucet is dripping badly again!

____

4. Don't you want to get it fixed now?

____

5. Oh, can you give me a ride? My car is still in the shop.

____

6. What kind of apartment are you interested in?

____

7. When do you need it?

____

8. May I come over tomorrow to take a look?

____

9. What time would you like to come?

____

10. May I have your name, please?

____

Storytelling (3)

Street

You've never been to Newton? Well, the centre's quite small. Main Street is the biggest street. It runs north-south. Then there's Old Street which is much smaller. As you go north up Main Street, Old Street is on the right. Opposite the junction of Simson Street and Goat Street, there's a big cinema.

Next to the cinema, there's a little cafe. It sells sweet coffee and ice-cream. There's a hotel with a large parking area beside it. Then opposite the hotel, there's a post office. If you go along Simson Street from Goat Street, the first shop on the right is a market. Then next to the market, there's a butcher. Opposite the butcher, there's a little baker's shop. I forgot the library. The library is on the south of New Street, on the corner with Broad Street.

Draw a map of the street matching the passages.

Grammar Exercises [3]

1. It's going to be the _____ exciting music festival today.
   ① much ② most
   ③ more ④ very

2. The longer the journey, _____ expensive the traffic fair.
   ① very ② the most
   ③ the more ④ much

3. We don't think that he is _____ diligent boy in his class.
   ① more ② much
   ③ the more ④ the most

4. The older you get, _____ difficult it becomes to find a job.
   ① more ② the more
   ③ the much more ④ the most

5. The value of sport is _____ greater than that of movie.
   ① very ② much
   ③ much more ④ far much more

6. A _____ explanation for the reason is necessary.
① farther ② farthest
③ further ④ furthest

7. She is good at tennis, but swimming is her _____ sport.
① the better favorite ② the most favorite
③ the best favorite ④ favorite

8. He is _____ man to tell a lie in the class.
① late ② latest
③ lately ④ the last

9. It is _____ in a restaurant than at home.
① expensive ② much expensive
③ more expensive ④ most expensive

10. The higher we go up, the _____ it becomes.
① colder ② much colder
③ more colder ④ most colder

Task Tips

elf-learning Strategies

Department ____________ Grade _____ Gender (Male, Female) Name (__)

Put a tick in the appropriate column.
(읽고 적절하다고 생각하는 칸에 표시하시오.)

	Strategies	Always	Often	Sometimes	Rarely	Never
1	I pay attention to the teacher.					
2	I took notes when I listen.					
3	I look notes when I read.					
4	I read the questions before I listen.					
5	I read the questions before I read.					
6	I look at my notes later.					
7	I repeat new words aloud.					
8	I use new words in a sentence.					
9	I look for information in a reference book.					
10	I do all my homework.					
11	I help a friend with homework.					
12	I ask the teacher questions.					
13	I ask a friend questions about schoolwork.					
14	I guess at new words.					

Chamot, O'Malley, & Kupper. (1992 : 98). In H. D. Brown(ed.), *Teaching by Principles : An interactive approach to language pedagogy. (2001).*

Unit 04

Busy Life

1. I Have a Pretty Tight Schedule Today.

Sara : Hi, George! Are you free now?
George : Yes, what's the matter?

Sara : Is it possible for us to have a talk sometime?
George : I'd love to, but I've got a pretty tight schedule today.

Sara : Oh, what are you going to do today?
George : Well, I should finish my English report by eleven.
After that, I'll have a meeting with my friends over lunch.

Sara : Oh, you have a tight schedule in the morning.
What about in the afternoon after lunch?
George : I think I finish lunch around two o'clock.
I won't have a break until two o'clock.

Sara : Are you free after two?

George : From two until five, I have to attend the English class.

Sara : Wow, you are really busy today.

2. I'm Not Able to Finish My Work.

Cathy : Jimmy, let's take a coffee break, shall we?
Jimmy : I wish I could, but I can't now.

Cathy : What keeps you so busy? You've been sitting there for hours.
Jimmy : Anyway, I'm sorry. I can't be with you now.

Cathy : You need to walk around for a while.
Don't just stay on the computer for a long time.
Jimmy : Sorry, I should finish my report.
My English professor needs it by noon.
I can't finish my work by the deadline.

Cathy : Oh, I understand that.
But just take a break over a cup of coffee.
You will feel better after a break.

3. Let's Take a Rest Today, Shall We?

Laura : We had a very good meeting, Samuel.
Samuel : Yes, I'm happy that we've finally finished our homework.

Laura : I think we have. Is there anything else to do?
Samuel : No, that's all. We solved all the problems, I guess.

Laura : What about the presentation for tourism management class? I think it will be a big assignment.
Samuel : Yes, it is not easy to prepare. But I'm so tired today.

Laura : Then, let's take a rest today, shall we?
Samuel : All right. That's a good idea.

Laura : Let's meet tomorrow afternoon, shall we?
Samuel : OK. See you later.

4. We Can Do It First in the Morning.

Nick : How many pages do we still need to finish?
We have been doing this all day.

Grace : We still have to do ten pages more.

Nick : Well, I'm tired from typing all the pages in the morning.

Grace : So am I. The typing is really boring work.

Nick : And it's about time to take a break for a while.

Grace : I know. But we'd better finish it by noon.

Nick : This work is not urgent. We can do it in the afternoon.

Grace : All right. Let's go to the cafeteria and have some coffee.

Nick : That's a good idea. Let's go there right away.

5. I'll Just Grab Something to Eat.

Simon : Where are you heading in such a hurry?

Judy : I'm heading home.

Simon : Are we still going to have group study tonight?

Judy : Right! I almost forgot. I'm really busy right now.
So, I will be a little late for the meeting.

Simon : Why? You should be on time.

Judy : I am very busy with a school project in the afternoon.
I don't even have time to sit down and enjoy a meal.

Simon : Do you have a presentation in the afternoon?

Judy : Yeah. I'm just going to grab something to eat.
And then I'll come back to school.

Simon : Oh, I see. See you then.

Judy : OK.

Review Exercises [Unit 4]

Read the sentence and write an appropriate answer.

1. Is it possible for us to have a talk sometime?

____

2. What are you going to do today?

____

3. Let's take a coffee break, shall we?

____

4. I think we have. Is there anything else to do?

____

5. What about the presentation for tourism management class?

____

6. Then, let's take a rest today, shall we?

____

7. Let's meet tomorrow afternoon, shall we?

____

8. How many pages do we need to finish?

____

9. I'm tired from typing all of the pages in the morning.

____

10. All right. Let's go to the cafeteria, and have some coffee.

____

Storytelling (4)

Fruits and Vegetables

I like sea food. I like fish very much. My favorite fish are tuna, oysters, shrimps, and crab, but I have never eaten raw fish. I have enjoyed eating meat since I was young, but I don't have it very often these days. So, I don't eat it often for a main dish. I sometimes eat pork, chicken, and beef. I don't like to eat lamb.

I like vegetables, but there's some vegetables I don't like. They're garlic and onions. I eat a lot of fruits everyone for breakfast, lunch, and dinner. I like most kinds of fruit very much. I usually eat apples, grapes, pears, but I don't like to eat pineapples at all.

Write some food for likes or dislikes.

Likes	Dislikes

Grammar Exercises [4]

1. This booklet contains information that workers _____ the goods.

① producing ② produce
③ productive ④ production

2. The playwright has _____ to convey the spirit of Shakespeare.

① labored ② understand
③ released ④ begged

3. Special prices offered by the airline _____ competitive.

① made ② explained
③ arranged ④ suggested

4. The messages you left _____ on my desk.

① have ② has
③ are ④ is

5. The court _____ the newspaper to pay me 5 hundred dollars.

① ordered ② studied
③ borrowed ④ changed

6. They have got _____ information of the election results.

① many ② some
③ so ④ few

7. There is _____ doubt about the effects of acid rain.

① many ② little
③ a few ④ few

8. There was _____ concern about energy shortages.

① a great deal of ② amounts of
③ many ④ a number of

9. The new prime minister has changed the country _____ .

① much ② many
③ little ④ a lot

10. She thinks that the shirt is much _____ .

① expensive ② more expensive
③ most expensive ④ the most expensive

Task Tips

Romanization of Korean

(1) Vowels

- simple vowels ________

ㅏ	ㅓ	ㅗ	ㅜ	ㅡ	ㅣ	ㅐ	ㅔ	ㅚ	ㅟ
a	eo	o	u	eu	i	ae	e	oe	wi

- diphthongs

ㅑ	ㅕ	ㅛ	ㅠ	ㅒ	ㅖ	ㅘ	ㅙ	ㅝ	ㅞ	ㅢ
ya	yeo	yo	yu	yae	ye	wa	wae	wo	we	ui

(2) Consonants

- plosives(stops) ________

ㄱ	ㄲ	ㅋ	ㄷ	ㄸ	ㅌ	ㅂ	ㅃ	ㅍ
g, k	kk	k	d, t	tt	t	b, p	pp	p

- affricates ________

ㅈ	ㅉ	ㅊ
j	jj	ch

- fricatives ________

ㅅ	ㅆ	ㅎ
s	ss	h

- nasals ________

ㄴ	ㅁ	ㅇ
n	m	ng

- liquids ________

ㄹ
r, l

Unit 05

Friends Helping Each Other

1. Something Might Have Happened.

Robert : Has Andy shown up?
Sandra : No, he has not yet. I guess something might have happened.

Robert : I wonder what happened.
Sandra : I don't know. I hope it's nothing serious.

Robert : Last week his sister went to the hospital.
Sandra : Oh, really? What happened?

Robert : His sister had a car accident last week.
Sandra : Is she fine now?

Robert : She's in the hospital, and she is still in a coma.
Sandra : Oh, poor Andy. I hope his sister is going to be better soon.

2. I Couldn't Help It.

Andy : What was that terrible noise?
Rosa : I'm sorry. I just dropped some dishes on the floor.

Andy : Oh, that's too bad. Were you hurt?
Rosa : Fortunately, no. I'm not hurt. But I'm terribly sorry.

Andy : I'm glad you're not hurt, but why did you drop the dishes?
Rosa : I couldn't help it. The dishes were too greasy and slippery.

Andy : Some dishes are greasy. You should be careful next time.
Rosa : Yes. Trust me. I will be careful.

3. I Hope It's Nothing Serious.

Cathy : Alex, are you coming to the party with us?
Alex : I wish I could, but something unexpected has happened.

Cathy : Oh, that's too bad. You look so worried. What's the problem?
Alex : I must go to see my professor this afternoon.

Cathy : I hope it's nothing serious.
Alex : Well, I guess it's just something personal.

Cathy : OK. But if you need any help, let me know.
Alex : Sure. I will.

Cathy : You can come to the party after you meet the professor.
Alex : I wish I could. I will call you after I see my professor.

4. He Went out of Business.

Andy : Have you heard that Mike went out of business?
Jane : Really? When did he go out of business?

Andy : Maybe last year.
Jane : That's too bad. He had owned the business for 10 years.
I wonder what happened to him.

Andy : I don't know exactly, but life must be pretty tough for him.
Jane : Well, I hope he will recover his business again.

Andy : I hope so.
Jane : We must give him help.

5. I Just Had an Interview Yesterday.

Ronald : Hi, Betty. I heard you're looking for a new job.
Betty : Yeah. I just had an interview yesterday.

Ronald : Oh. How was it? Did you do well?
Betty : I think I did well.
They said they would make a decision by next week.

Ronald : By next week?
I hope they will hire a person like you.
Betty : Yeah, I hope so, too.

Ronald : What's your application for a job?
Betty : I believe they seem to like me.

Ronald : Well, you may have a good chance.
Betty : Thanks. I hope so.

Review Exercises [Unit 5]

Read the sentence and write an appropriate answer.

1. What was that terrible noise?

   ____

2. Oh, that's too bad. Were you hurt?

   ____

3. But why did you drop the plates?

   ____

4. You should be careful next time.

   ____

5. Are you coming to the party with us?

6. You look so worried. What's the problem?

7. I hope it's nothing serious.

8. But if you need help, let me know.

9. Hi! I heard you're looking for a new job.

10. How was it? Did you do it well?

Storytelling (5)

Sports

I like a game of table tennis with my friends on weekends, so I'm quite good at it. However, I don't like tennis and baseball at all. I'm terrible at tennis and baseball game. In the summer, I love summer and I like swimming, especially in the sea. I love playing badminton but I'm not very good at it though I practise it a lot. Other main sports are volley ball and basketball in the field. I really enjoy them after class or on weekends. My sister is interested in chess, so she is sometimes trying to get me to play, but I hate it. Other favorite hobbies are climbing mountain and taking a walk alone.

Write some sports and hobbies for likes or dislikes.

Likes	Dislikes

Grammar Exercises [5]

1. The company hires the employees _____ work for new project.
   ① which ② who's
   ③ whose ④ who

2. The jewel _____ was very valuable was given to the museum.
   ① which ② who
   ③ whose ④ as

3. He always likes the man _____ is right.
   ① who ② as
   ③ that ④ what

4. Yesterday she met a reporter _____ worked at a newspaper.
   ① as ② that
   ③ who ④ but

5. He was out of town on the day _____ the accident happened.
   ① which ② how
   ③ that ④ when

6. We are always delighted to see the man _____ we love.

① who ② which

③ whom ④ whose

7. The most valuable thing _____ people can have is time.

① where ② what

③ that ④ how

8. We can find lots of books _____ are instructive for research.

① where ② when

③ who ④ which

9. I think the boy _____ lives next door works in bank.

① whom ② who

③ which ④ whose

10. A boy and his cat _____ were passing by were injured.

① that ② which

③ whom ④ who

Task Tips

The Phonemic Chart

VOWELS / DIPHTHONGS

i:	ɪ	ʊ	u:	ɪə	eɪ	
green	pink	wood	blue	clear	grey	
ɛ	ə	ɜ:	ɔ:	ʊə	ɔɪ	oʊ
red	silver	purple	fawn	pure white	turquoise	yellow
æ	ʌ	ɑ:	ɒ	ɛə	ɑɪ	ɑʊ
black	rust	khaki	orange	fair	sky blue	brown

CONSONANTS

p	b	t	d	tʃ	dʒ	k	g
Poland	Burma	Thailand	Denmark	China	Germany	Korea	Greenland
f	v	θ	ð	s	z	ʃ	ʒ
France	Vietnam	South Africa	The Philipines	Singapore	Zambia	Russia	Malaysia
m	n	ŋ	h	l	r	w	j
Mexico	Norway	Hong Kong	Hungary	Laos	Romania	Wales	Yugoslavia

http://www.google.co.kr/imgres?q=pronounce+mouth&start=100&hl=ko&newwindow

Unit 06

Studying and Tests

1. Everything Will Be Fine.

Bob : Rose, you look so worried. What happened?

Rose : Well, I want to take that class.
But there were so many students on the waiting list.

Bob : So many students on the waiting list? Don't worry so much.

Rose : I think chances are probably slim for me.

Bob : I wouldn't say that! Many students may drop the class.
And then there will be some openings.

Rose : Really? Are you sure?

Bob : You may get a chance for the class.

Rose : I hope so.

Bob : Come on. Cheer up. Everything will be fine.

2. Let's Try to Comfort Her.

Jason : You look so concerned, Dolly. What's the matter with you?
Dolly : I'm worried about the interview tomorrow.
It's so important to me.

Jason : Don't you have some experience?
Dolly : You know, I've been looking for a job for three months.
This is my first interview.

Jason : I can help you. I will teach you some strategies for interview.
Dolly : Really? Are you sure?

Jason : Don't worry too much, Dolly. Everything will be fine.
Dolly : I hope so.

Jason : Come on, Dolly. Let's keep our fingers crossed.
Dolly : What does it mean?

Jason : It just means "good luck."

3. You Look So Worried.

Sara : Phil! You look so worried. What's the matter?

Phil : I have a big problem. I will have an English exam this week. But I haven't prepared it yet.

Sara : Well, don't worry too much. You still have two days.

Phil : I know but two days are not enough for an English exam. I have another exam tomorrow.

Sara : Don't worry. I will help you. I have some summary notes.

Phil : Can I borrow the copies?

Sara : Of course. I will copy them for you.

Phil : Thank you. You are so generous.

Sara : You're welcome. We are good friends.

4. I Have a Presentation Next Week.

Sara : Jimmy, you look so tired. What happened?
Jimmy : I didn't sleep well last night.

Sara : Did you have something on your mind? You look so worried.
Jimmy : Yes, I have a big problem recently.

Sara : That's too bad. Maybe I can help you.
Jimmy : Well, I'm under a lot of pressure.
I have a presentation for the class next week.
But I haven't finished all of my projects.

Sara : Is there anything I can do to help you?
Jimmy : Well, I guess no one can help me. I will try to do it for myself.

Sara : But I can do something for you.
Jimmy : Thanks. You're so kind.

5. He Failed the Test.

Andy : Have you heard that Mike failed the test?

Jane : Really? What subject did he take?

Andy : Maybe, it's English conversation.

Jane : That's too bad. He studied hard for the course.
Why did he fail the test?

Andy : I don't know exactly.
But they said he was late for the test.
Unfortunately he went to the wrong class for the test.

Jane : Oh, he had a terrible experience.
Well, I hope he will study hard again next semester.

Andy : I hope so.

Review Exercises [Unit 6]

Read the sentence and write an appropriate answer.

1. You look so worried. What happened?

____

2. You may get a chance for the class.

____

3. What's the matter with you?

____

4. Don't you have some experiences?

____

5. I will teach you some strategies for interview.

____

6. What does it mean?

____

7. Can I borrow the copies?

____

8. You look so tired. What happened?

____

9. Did you have something on your mind?

____

10. Is there anything I can do to help you?

____

Storytelling (6)

Housework

My aunt lives on her own, and her house is a really messy house. Last weekends I went to see her and I spent the whole day doing her housework for her. First of all, I sweep the whole house, and then I washed her dishes. She tried to stop me. She said that she always polished her dishes every day. She said that she could manage by herself. She said that she made meal everyday by herself. She tries to shop on Fridays. She usually cleans the clothes. On Monday, she cleans the bathroom and livingroom. But she never do any housework on weekends. She just stay home and takes a full rest for a long time.

Write her weekly work in the house.

Grammar Exercises [6]

1. They will be _____ unprepared for the new project or unwilling to make a decision.

① both ② for
③ either ④ as

2. _____ people in the town are responsible for the pollution.

① A lot of ② plenty
③ much ④ crowd

3. Concerning the cause of the fire, many _____ have been raised.

① concentrations ② influences
③ questions ④ flames

4. Most of _____ asked the employer to invest for the company.

① employ ② employee
③ employer ④ employees

5. There is no _____ that the manager will move to another branch.

① management ② news
③ loyalty ④ technology

6. I have no meeting with anyone who _____ power.

① was ② has

③ have ④ were

7. One third of all participants _____ the meeting today.

① was attended ② attended

③ has attended ④ attending

8. _____ of them likes Jimmy because he is so picky.

① Either ② Both

③ All ④ Neither

9. It _____ hot in summer last year.

① is ② are

③ was ④ were

10. The early bird usually _____ the worm.

① catch ② catches

③ catched ④ caught

Task Tips

American English Monophthongs

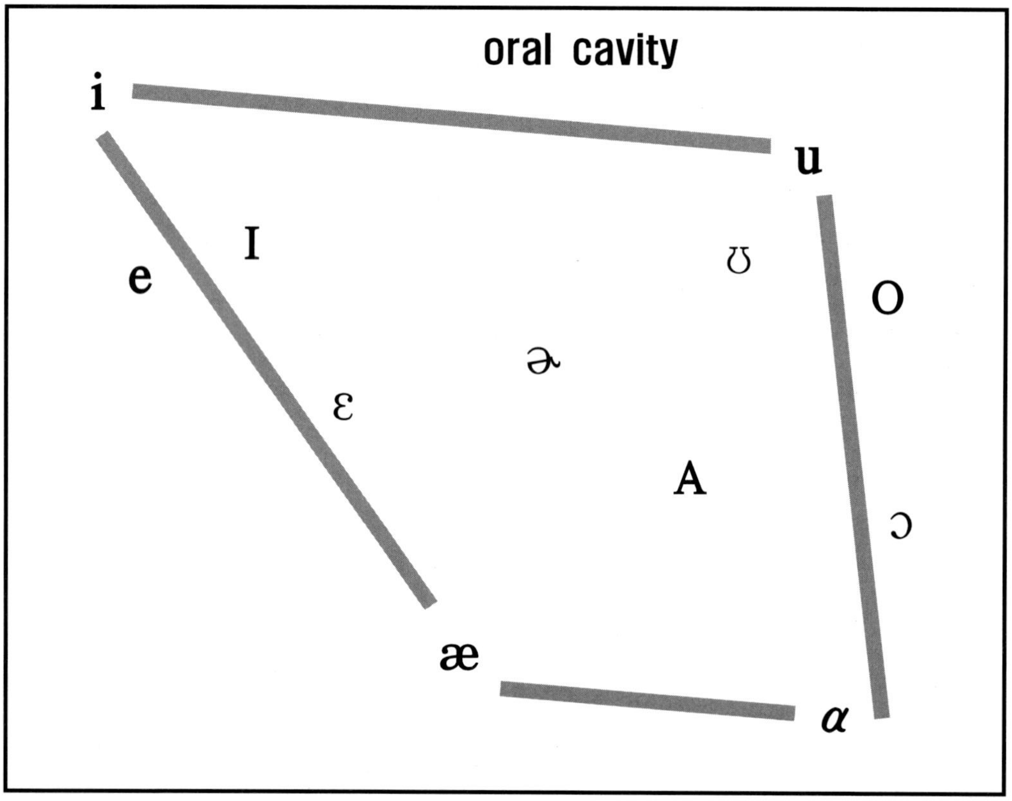

Unit 07

An Unforgettable Experience

1. Do You Have Anything in Mind?

Daniel : I sent out the invitations for my birthday party.
Molly : That's good. Now what should we do?

Daniel : We should plan the menu.
Molly : Oh, that's right. Do you have anything in mind?

Daniel : I think I'm going to make the chicken salad.
I know the recipe.
Molly : Yeah, but did you forget that Grace doesn't eat chicken?

Daniel : Grace? Oh, my God! I forgot to invite her.
She'll be mad at me. That's my mistake.
Molly : Well, it's not too late yet. I'll make a phone call. Don't worry.

Daniel : Thanks. I think I sometimes forget important things.
Molly : Don't worry. Everybody makes mistake.

2. I Was Locked out of My Apartment Last Night.

Matthew : I had something terrible last night.
Jane : Did you have anything wrong? What's the matter?

Matthew : I was locked out of my apartment last night.
Jane : How did that happen? Did you lose your keys?

Matthew : No. I left the keys in my room.
Jane : Then how did you get in?

Matthew : I climbed in from the window. It was terrible.
Jane : What? Oh, my god!
You climbed the wall and got in. You're so brave.

Matthew : Thanks. But I was so scared.
Anyway, I won't do it again.
Jane : Yes. Never do it again.

3. I Can't Find Her Number.

Margaret : Do you know what Jane's home phone number is?

Peter : I can't think of it at all. You'd better look it up in the phone book.

Margaret : I've checked it already. But I can't find her number. Sorry.

Peter : Maybe it's somewhere else, I think.

Margaret : Well, I guess so.

Peter : Maybe you can call her friends and ask her number.

Margaret : I already tried. But her friends didn't tell me.
They said they didn't know her number.

Peter : Oh, that's too bad.
They usually don't release private information over the phone.

Margaret : We try to find other ways.

4. You Are behind the Times.

Tony : Your dress looks funny.
Sara : I don't think so. It looks fine to me.

Tony : Are you kidding? You are behind the times.
That style went out last year.
Sara : Oh, come on. I think it looks good on me.

Tony : Wow, you're really out-dated.
Sara : Well, you're right. I'm out of style. I will change my style.

Tony : Good. If you change your dress, it will look good on you.
Sara : Thanks for your suggestion.

Review Exercises [Unit 7]

Read the sentence and write an appropriate answer.

1. Now what should we do?

____

2. Do you have anything in mind?

____

3. Did you have anything wrong? What's the matter?

____

4. Did you lose your keys?

____

5. Then how did you get in?

____

6. Do you know what Jane's home phone number is?

____

7. I've checked it already. But I can't find her number.

____

8. Your dress looks funny.

____

9. You are behind the times. That style went out last year.

____

10. If you change your dress, it will look good on you.

____

Storytelling [7]

Direction : Finding a Way

1) Go along the path until you get to the river.
2) Go through the wood until you come to a river.
3) At the bottom of the hill is a small lake.
4) In front of you there is a mountain.
5) Climb the mountain.
6) Cross the river and turn left at the lake. Go round the lake.
7) Go across the bridge and walk along the bank of the river.
8) Come to a small wood and go through the wood.
9) Walk along the bank of the river for about fifteen minutes.
10) Come to a small bridge.
11) You'll swim to the island of a lake.
12) The treasure is under a rock on top of the mountain.

1. Arrange the directions as you walk along the way.

2. Draw a map and indicate the positions from directions.

Grammar Exercises [7]

1. I learned that three and five _____ eight.
   ① make ② made
   ③ got ④ gotten

2. I know that our school bus _____ at 8 this evening.
   ① arriving ② arrived
   ③ has arrived ④ will arrive

3. The Second World War _____ out in 1939.
   ① break ② breaking
   ③ broke ④ has broke

4. There are _____ in her room, and she likes them.
   ① five furnitures ② five piece of furniture
   ③ five pieces of furniture ④ five pieces of furnitures

5. The students took great _____ to finish the project.
   ① pain ② pains
   ③ paining ④ painings

6. Most of _____ are going to the family meeting.

① relative ② relatives

③ relativing ④ relation

7. A lot of computers _____ sold in the techno-mark.

① is ② are

③ being ④ was

8. There _____ a lot of computers in the store.

① is ② are

③ be ④ are to

9. I met some friends whovat the seminar last year.

① is ② are

③ was ④ were

10. All professors in the department _____ the meeting yesterday.

① attend ② attends

③ attended ④ attending

Task Tips

English Speaking Countries

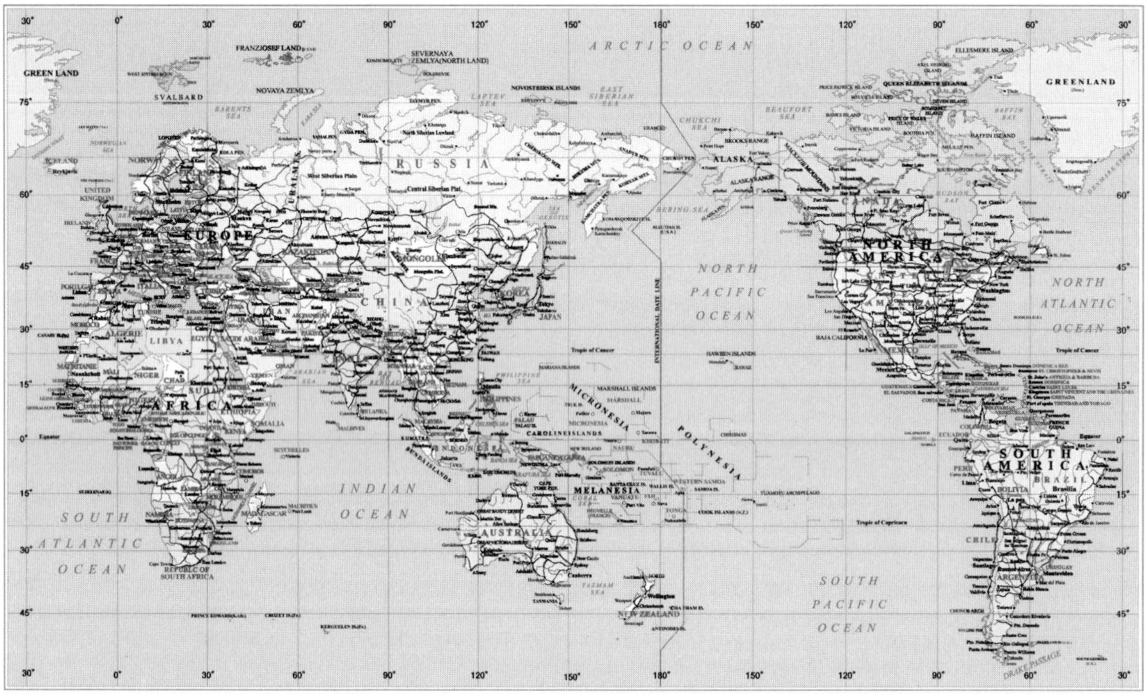

http://www.google.co.kr/imgres?q=English+speaking+countries&hl=ko&newwindow

Unit 08

Money and Change

1. Can You Break a Twenty-dollar Bill?

Cashier : Good afternoon, sir. How can I help you?
Customer : Could you break a 20 for me?

Cashier : Sure. How do you want it?
Customer : Could I have two 5's and the rest in ones?

Cashier : Well, I have some 5's, but I don't have enough 1's. Are quarters fine with you?
Customer : Oh, that's even better. I also need some quarters.

Cashier : Good, here you go.
Customer : Thank you.

2. I Have Change for a Dollar.

Jane : Do you have change for a dollar, please?
Brian : Yes, I do have some. What do you need it for?

Jane : I need some change for the bus.
Brian : How do you want it?

Jane : I need a couple of quarters and five dimes.
Brian : Sure. You need two quarters and five dimes.
Here you are.

Jane : Thanks. You are my true friend.

3. I Have Some Coins for Change.

Sandra : Excuse me?

Cashier : Yes, can I help you?

Sandra : Yes. I need to get some change for the parking meter.
May I have change for a five dollar bill?

Cashier : How would you like it?

Sandra : I just need five dollars in quarters.

Cashier : I'm sorry, but we're not allowed to give change.

Sandra : Oh, that's too bad.
Is there a change machine somewhere around here?

Cashier : There is one in the shopping mall across the street.

Sandra : Well, that's too far.

4. I Have Just Lost a Coin.

Anne : Oh, I have just lost a coin in this vending machine.
Sam : I'm not surprised. It's always out of order.

Anne : Yeah. It just eats my money.
Sam : OK. Let me try. Whenever it doesn't work, just hit it. And it'll work.

Anne : You mean, I hit the machine like this.
Sam : Yes, you can just knock it like this. It sometimes works.

Anne : But I don't like to make a noise.
Sam : Well, what will you do? Do you have other way?

Anne : Let's put a sign on it so that the same thing may not happen.
Sam : That's a good idea.

5. I'm out of Coins.

Mary : Oh, that's terrible. The washing machine is out of order again.

Peter : You can try anothcr onc. That onc works.

Mary : But I'm out of coins.

Peter : Did you press the coin release lever?

Mary : Yes, but nothing happened. I didn't get any return.
I will complain to the manager.

Peter : It sometimes doesn't work these days.

Mary : Yes, this has happened so many times.

Review Exercises [Unit 8]

Read the sentence and write an appropriate answer.

1. Good afternoon, sir. How can I help you?

____

2. Sure. How do you want it?

____

3. Do you have change for a dollar, please?

____

4. What do you need it for?

____

5. I'm sorry, but we're not allowed to give change.

____

6. Is there a change machine somewhere around here?

____

7. I have just lost a coin in this vending machine.

____

8. You mean, I hit the machine like this.

____

9. You can just knock it like this. It sometimes works.

____

10. Well, what will you do? Do you have other way?

____

Storytelling (8)

Kinds of Job

(A) I start my work at ten pm. I put on my uniform then I go up to the ward. First of all there is a meeting to discuss the patients, then I go round the ward to check all the patients. After that, it depends! Some nights are very quiet, some are very busy. Sometimes I have to deal with emergencies. I finish work at six in the morning and go home just as everyone go to bed. It's a hard Job, but I like working with people.

(B) I start work at five in the morning. It's a very busy Job. First of all I have to milk the cows, then I feed all the other animals. Then I go to the fields. My job depends on the season. In spring I have to plough the fields and sow the seed, then in summer I have to do the weeding. Autumn is very busy because that's harvest time. In winter I can relax for a while. I enjoy working outdoors.

(C) My job starts at six in the morning. First I have to go to the main office to sort the letters for my round. Then at about half past seven, I get on my bicycle with my bag of letters and go round the houses. It's a nice job. I know everyone on my round and they're always pleased to see me, especially the old people. They love to get letters. I deliver letters until about ten, then I go back to the office and sort letters again.

Write the job as explained in the passages.

(A)

(B)

(C)

Grammar Exercises [8]

1. I _____ fifteen years old next year.
   ① will ② will be
   ③ being ④ am

2. When the messenger _____ , she will give it to him.
   ① will arrive ② arrive
   ③ arrives ④ arrived

3. They say that she _____ her mother.
   ① resemble ② resembles
   ③ is resembling ④ will resemble

4. He _____ the president of the country since 2005.
   ① has been ② was
   ③ will be ④ has being

5. Have you ever _____ the movie?
   ① see ② saw
   ③ seen ④ will see

6. It _____ every day for two weeks.

① rains ② rained

③ is raining ④ has rained

7. A good idea _____ to me when I was walking along the path.

① occur ② occurring

③ occurred ④ will occur

8. He _____ the sales representative of the company last year.

① is ② was

③ will be ④ had been

9. I _____ my homework by five o'clock this evening.

① finish ② have finished

③ finished ④ will have finished

10. He hope that he _____ a job after his graduation.

① is ② will get

③ have got ④ would get

Task Tips

List of English Speaking Countries (2005)

Country	Region	Population
Antigua and Barbuda	Caribbean	85,000
Australia	Australia	22,374,370
Bahamas, The	Caribbean	331,000
Barbados	Caribbean	294,000
Belize	Central America / Caribbean	288,000
Botswana	Africa	1,882,000
Cameroon	Africa	18,549,000
Canada	North America	33,531,000
Dominica	Caribbean	73,000
Eritrea	Africa	5,224,000
Ethiopia	Africa	82,101,998
Fiji	Oceania	827,900
The Gambia	Africa	1,709,000
Ghana	Africa	23,478,000
Grenada	Caribbean	106,000
Guyana	South America / Caribbean	738,000
India	Asia	1,143,540,000
Ireland	Europe	4,581,269
Jamaica	Caribbean	2,714,000
Kenya	Africa	37,538,000
Kiribati	Oceania	95,000
Kingdom of the Netherlands	Caribbean (and Europe)	17,000,000
Lesotho	Africa	2,008,000
Liberia	Africa	3,750,000
Malawi	Africa	13,925,000
Malta	Europe	412,600
Marshall Islands	Oceania	59,000
Mauritius	Africa / Indian Ocean	1,262,000
Federated States of Micronesia	Oceania	111,000

Country	Region	Population
Namibia	Africa	2,074,000
Nauru	Oceania	10,000
New Zealand	Oceania	4,294,350
Nigeria	Africa	148,093,000
Pakistan	Asia	165,449,000
Palau	Oceania	20,000
Papua New Guinea	Oceania	6,331,000
Philippines	Asia	90,457,200
Rwanda	Africa	9,725,000
Saint Kitts and Nevis	Caribbean	50,000
Saint Lucia	Caribbean	165,000
Saint Vincent and the Grenadines	Caribbean	120,000
Samoa	Oceania	188,359
Seychelles	Africa / Indian Ocean	87,000
Sierra Leone	Africa	5,866,000
Singapore	Asia	4,839,400
Solomon Islands	Oceania	506,992
South Africa	Africa	47,850,700
South Sudan	Africa	8,260,490
Sudan	Africa	31,894,000
Swaziland	Africa	1,141,000
Tanzania	Africa	40,454,000
Tonga	Oceania	100,000
Trinidad and Tobago	Caribbean	1,333,000
Tuvalu	Oceania	11,000
The United Kingdom	Europe	61,612,300
The United States	North America	309,442,000
Uganda	Africa	30,884,000
Vanuatu	Oceania	226,000
Zambia	Africa	11,922,000
Zimbabwe	Africa	13,349,000

Unit 09

Shopping at a Store

1. Do You Have These Kinds of Shoes?

Clerk : Good afternoon. How may I help you?
Ken : Yes. Do you have these kinds of shoes?

Clerk : Let see. What size do you want?
Ken : Do you have them in size six?

Clerk : I'm not sure. You can look for them on the rack.
Ken : I see. I will look for the size.

Clerk : If you can't find them on the rack, they may be out of stock. But let me look in the stockroom.
Ken : Thanks. I'd like to try on a pair of shoes if you have them.

Clerk : I'll be back and show them to you.

2. That's a Rip-off.

Donald : Hi, Annie! I bought a new shirt at a market.
Annie : It looks pretty. How much did you pay for it?

Donald : I paid 20,000 won for this shirt.
Annie : 20,000 won just for the shirt? I think that's a rip-off.

Donald : What do you mean?
Annie : It's not worth it. You paid too much for it.

Donald : Do you think I paid too much for the price?
Annie : Yes, you sure did. They got too much money from you.

Donald : Oh, that's too expensive. I really got ripped off.

3. I Am Just Browsing Now.

George : Good afternoon. May I help you?
Susan : No, thanks. I'm just browsing.

George : You are just looking around, aren't you?
Susan : Yes, I am. I'm just browsing now.

George : All right. If you need any help, just let me know.
Susan : Sure. I'll let you know if I need help.

George : Enjoy looking around.
Susan : Well, this small bed is very cute. A baby will like it.

George : You're right. This baby bed is a very good brand.
Susan : Is it firm and comfortable?

George : You don't have to worry about its quality.
Susan : That's an attractive one. I'll think about it.

4. We Can Do Window Shopping.

Sam : Emily, the shopping mall is going to have a big sale today.
Do you want to go there with me?

Emily : Oh, really? That's a good chance, but I don't feel like it.

Sam : Why? We can buy something for a cheap price.

Emily : I'm sorry. I can't go there. I'm broke.

Sam : I see. But we can do some window shopping there.

Emily : Just look around? Good, but that's boring.

Sam : Cheer up, and go with me.

Emily : Yes, I will go and do window shopping.

Sam : That's a good idea. Hurry up.

5. Keep the Receipt, Please.

Cashier : Is there anything else?

Jimmy : Excuse me?

Cashier : Is there anything else you would like to buy?

Jimmy : No, thank you. I think that's all.

Cashier : Anything for help?

Jimmy : Can I return it if it has any problem?

Cashier : Yes. But you must return it within two weeks.

Jimmy : By the way, is there a charge for that?

Cashier : No. There will be no charge at all.
However, you must show us the receipt.

Jimmy : Yes, I see.

Cashier : Keep your receipt.
If something comes up, you can show it to us.
And we'll give you a refund.

Jimmy : Thanks.

Review Exercises [Unit 9]

Read the sentence and write an appropriate answer.

1. Do you have this kind of shoes?

____

2. Do you have them in size six?

____

3. You can look for them on the rack.

____

4. How much did you pay for it?

____

5. Do you think I paid too much for the price?

____

6. You are just looking around, aren't you?

____

7. If you need any help, just let me know.

____

8. Is it firm and comfortable?

____

9. Do you want to go there with me?

____

10. Why? We can buy something for a cheap price.

____

Storytelling (9)

Daily Schedule

Today I'm going to have a lot of classes at college all day. In the morning I have three classes and another three classes in the afternoon. Before I attend the class, I will drop to the group meeting room to talk about the presentation. I will have lunch with friends at a school cafeteria at 12:00. I will go to the library after classes at 4:00 in the afternoon. At 7:00 in the evening, I'm going to watch football game. Before the game, I'm going to walk to the market and buy some food. On the way to the market, I'm going to meet my friend Hyesong. At around ten, I'm going to arrive at home and study my homework for tomorrow classes.

Fill the time and schedule in the list.

Time	Schedule
12:00	Lunch with friends

Grammar Exercises [9]

1. I learned that honesty _____ always the best policy.
   ① is ② was
   ③ be ④ will be

2. The president _____ a short speech at the meeting.
   ① made ② took
   ③ told ④ said

3. I am going to _____ to The Philippines this winter.
   ① go a trip ② take a trip
   ③ come a trip ④ become a trip

4. I admire him because he never _____ a lie.
   ① says ② tells
   ③ talks ④ speaks

5. I have never expected to _____ my living as a writer.
   ① have ② having
   ③ earning ④ earn

6. The team will get a chance _____ to the Olympic Games.

① to travel ② traveling

③ for traveling ④ to have travelled

7. She likes a student with short hair to _____ along with others.

① it ② along

③ one ④ get

8. She usually makes it a rule _____ the class on time.

① attend ② attending

③ to attend ④ to be attended

9. She had a hard time in _____ the subject last semester.

① study ② studied

③ studying ④ to be studied

10. During the course, the textbook is too difficult for him _____.

① read ② reading

③ to read ④ to be read

Task Tips

Language Functions in a Brain

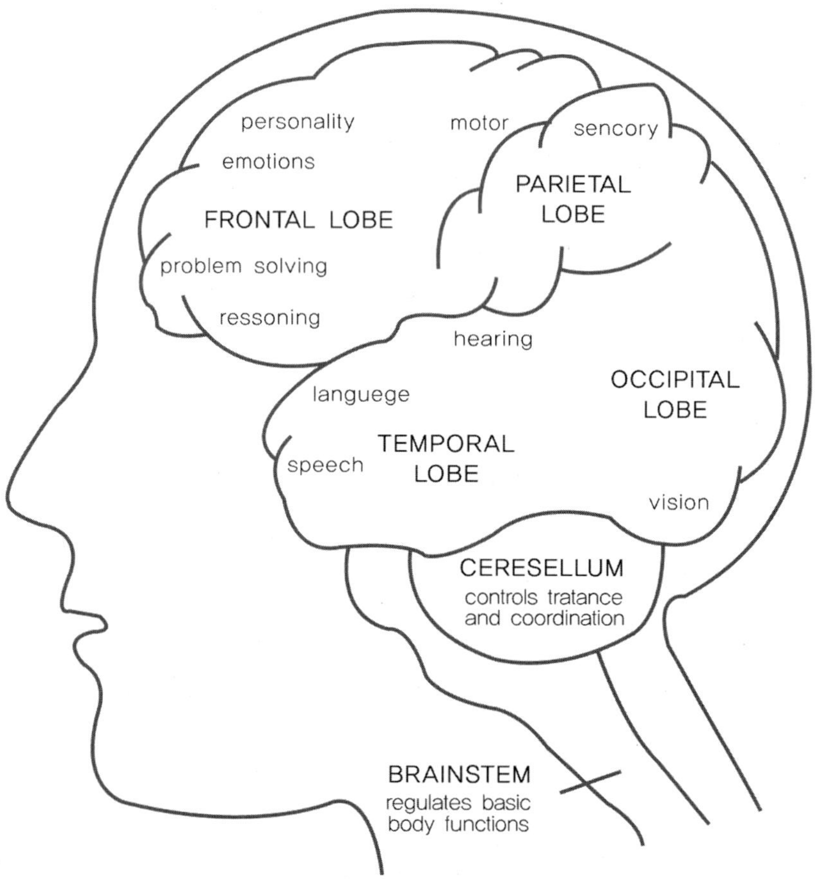

Unit 10

Time and Schedule

1. I'm Going to Invite My Friends.

Andy : Ellis, what are you going to do this weekends?
Ellis : This weekend?

Andy : Yeah, I am thinking of inviting you and some friends.
Ellis : Oh, that would be fine.

Andy : Can you come to my house for dinner?
Ellis : I'm sorry. I will be busy this weekend.

Andy : Do you have any other plans?
Ellis : Yes, I have already had made an appointment with Julia. I will study for my assignment with her.

Andy : Oh, right. Well, maybe some other time.
Ellis : Yes, some other time. Sorry.

2. I Want to Make an Appointment with Him.

Receptionist : Hello! This is Kookje Corporation. May I help you?

Steve : Yes. This is Mr. Steve Jackson from ABC Tourism Agency. May I speak to Mrs. Jeong?

Receptionist : I'm sorry. She is not in now. She is out of town this afternoon.

Steve : Could I make an appointment to see her tomorrow?

Receptionist : Well, let me see. She will be busy tomorrow. She has some appointments tomorrow morning.

Steve : What about tomorrow afternoon? Is she available?

Receptionist : That will be fine. What time do you want?

Steve : I would like to see her around three.

Receptionist : OK. Please come to see her at three tomorrow.

Steve : Good, thank you.

3. My Alarm Clock Didn't Work This Morning.

Ellis : I'm really sorry. I overslept.

Frank : Why? Why do you late for the class?

Ellis : My alarm clock didn't work this morning.

Frank : Again this morning?

Ellis : That's right. I did set the alarm last night.

Frank : Your clock never works.
Umm ... , you should buy a new one.

Ellis : Well, if it doesn't work again tomorrow, I'll buy a new one.

Frank : I think you should buy a new one today.

Ellis : Why?

Frank : The clock may not work tomorrow.

4. My Watch Gains 10 Minutes Everyday.

Bob : My watch always gains ten minutes a day.
Molly : That's funny. I have a similar problem.

Bob : What do you mean?
Molly : My watch always loses ten minutes a day.

Bob : No kidding.
Molly : I'm serious. Every morning I set my watch by the radio. But it still loses ten minutes everyday.

Bob : It really disturbs you, doesn't it?
Molly : Yes, I think I will buy a new one.

Bob : You'd better buy a new one today.

Review Exercises [Unit 10]

Read the sentence and write an appropriate answer.

1. What are you going to do this weekends?

___

2. Can you come to my house for dinner?

___

3. Do you have any plan to do?

___

4. Hello! This is Kookje Corporation. May I help you?

___

5. May I speak to Mrs. Jeong?

6. Could I make an appointment to see her tomorrow?

7. What about tomorrow afternoon? Is it available?

8. What time do you want?

9. Why do you late for the class?

10. Umm you should buy a new one.

Storytelling [10]

Summer Vacation

My student, Haesong, was to spend a summer vacation with me. She and my daughter were the same age. We took them to the beach and enjoyed swimming. We went to the mountain near the beach. I had not realized that there were a lot of rocks and trees in the woods. About three hours later, the two girls came back to my cottage, with their tired eyes. Haesong had slipped on the path in the woods and my daughter managed to hold her back from the woods. I felt afraid that I had been blindly irresponsible, but nothing serious happened for her. There was no need to go to the hospital. I think that it was fortunate for us at that time.

1. Tell the story to your friends.

2. Write the story again by changing some words or expressions.

Grammar Exercises [10]

1. Traffic jam made _____ difficult for people to go through the road.
   ① it　　② themselves
   ③ one　　④ them

2. _____ will not be easy to reduce air pollution in the city.
   ① He　　② One
   ③ They　　④ It

3. Without others' help, she is developing new program _____ .
   ① by herself　　② on her
   ③ between herself　　④ her own

4. People claim that smoking damage _____ health.
   ① you　　② your
   ③ yourself　　④ yourselves

5. The climate of this country is similar to _____ of Vietnam.
   ① this　　② that
   ③ those　　④ it

6. I found that _____ completed the project for herself.

① she ② her

③ hers ④ herself

7. She enjoys the work _____ and don't complains any more.

① oncsclf ② herself

③ itself ④ himself

8. The owner evenly distributed the income to .

① one ② him

③ another ④ others

9. This cell phone isn't working well. So, please give me _____ .

① other ② others

③ another ④ more

10. Did you answer _____ questions in the job interview?

① all ② each

③ every ④ another

Task Tips

English Learning Motivation

	English Learning Motivation
1	I study English hard because I want to be rewarded by parents.
2	I study English hard because I want to be praised by others.
3	I study English hard because I want to get good grade.
4	I study English hard because I want to be easy in my course.
5	I study English hard because I want to get a good job in the future.
6	I study English hard because I want to enter the university.
7	I study English hard because I want to apply for school grant.
8	I study English hard because I want to know something new.
9	I study English hard because I want to understand more English.
10	I study English hard because I want to travel foreign countries.
11	I study English hard because I want to solve difficult problems.
12	I study English hard because I want to get more information.
13	I study English hard because I want to listen and speak in English.
14	I study English hard because I want to know various cultures and people.

Revised based on Gardner (1985). *Social psychology and second language learning : The role of attitudes and motivation. London : Edward Arnold.*

Unit 11

Traffic

1. My Car Broke Down.

Bob : Why didn't you show up for class this morning?
Karen : I don't want to talk about it. I had a terrible problem.

Bob : What happened?
Karen : This morning my car broke down.

Bob : Oh, that's terrible. What was it?
Karen : The engine seemed to be old. It sometimes makes me crazy.

Bob : Wow. Have you thought about getting a new car?
Karen : Yeah, I've thought about that, but I can't afford a new car.

Bob : Maybe that's a problem.
And then, you can take a bus or a subway for your safety.
Karen : Yeah, I will take a subway.

Bob : Good idea.

2. My Computer Is a Piece of Junk.

Cony : Hi, I just heard you bought a new computer last week.
Andrew : Yes. But unfortunately, it seemed to be a junk.

Cony : Excuse me?
Andrew : I think it turned out to be a piece of junk.

Cony : What do you mean?
Andrew : I bought the computer for two hundred dollars.
But it doesn't work.

Cony : Is that so? Then why did you buy it?
Andrew : It worked well when I bought it.

Cony : Oh, no. I think you were ripped off.
Andrew : What do you mean?

Cony : You paid too much for the wrong one.
Andrew : Oh, my god! You are right.

3. You Ran Through the Stop Sign.

John : Ma'am, did I do anything wrong?

Officer : Yes. You ran through the stop sign.
May I see your driver license, please?

John : Oh, I'm sorry. I didn't see the stop sign.

Officer : That doesn't justify your violation.
May I see your license, please?

John : Oh, I'm sorry, ma'am. I don't have it on me.
I forgot it back at the house.

Officer : No, you are wrong. You should have it.

John : But I have the insurance policy with me.
Here it is, officer.

Officer : Please wait here, sir. I'll come back in a moment.

4. I Make a Right Turn on a Red Light.

Officer : Excuse me, sir. Didn't you see the red light?
Jimmy : Oh, I thought I could make a right turn on red.

Officer : No, sir. The sign says "No Turn on Red."
Jimmy : Oh, I didn't see it.

Officer : I'm sorry, sir.
May I see your driver's license and insurance policy, please?
I have to give you a ticket.
Jimmy : Here they are.

Officer : Sign here, please.
Jimmy : What can I do, officer?

Officer : You can appeal to the court within 14 days.
Please drive safely, sir.
Jimmy : Thank you, Ma'am.

5. Traffic Is Bumper to Bumper

Ronald : I heard you are going to Seoul this evening.
Jane : Yes. I am. I will have a meeting with my friends there.

Ronald : Well, you may not know this. It's Christmas tomorrow. So, everybody stops work early today.
Jane : Do you mean we will have a traffic problem?

Ronald : That's right. Today they can go back home early.
Jane : How will it be?

Ronald : Traffic usually becomes bumper to bumper.
Jane : Oh, I didn't know that. Well, I'll leave a little early today.

Ronald : That will be better. Leave as early as possible.

6. The Traffic Was Crawling.

Kate : Oh, my god! The traffic is crawling.
Max : I think there's a traffic accident ahead.

Kate : We're now running late.
Max : I know. Why don't we take a different route?

Kate : Let me take a look at the map.
Max : Did you find any other route?

Kate : Yes, there's an exit two miles ahead.
We'll exit Maple Street, and then get on Paramatta Road.
Max : OK, let's take the road.

Kate : But we may take a longer way.
Max : It doesn't matter. That's a shortcut.

Review Exercises [Unit 11]

Read the sentence and write an appropriate answer.

1. Why didn’t you show up for class this morning?

____

2. What happened?

____

3. Have you thought about getting a new car?

____

4. And then, you take a bus or a subway for your safety.

____

5. I just heard you bought a new computer last week.

____

6. What do you mean?

____

7. Then why did you buy it?

____

8. You paid too much for the wrong one.

____

9. May I see your driver license, please?

____

10. I don't have it on me. I forgot it back at the house.

____

Storytelling [11]

Family Members

Mary comes from a large family. She lives with her mother and father, two brothers, and sisters. Her father's name is Jimmy. He's 51 years old. Her mother's name is Margaret. She's 48 years old. Mary's grandparents lives with them, too. They're quite old now. Her grandmother is 76 and her grandfather is 78. Mary has two brothers. They are Sam and Jack. Her grandparents has other one daughter and one son. Jane is Mary's aunts. Mary's husband is Bob, and they have two children. Fred is Mary's uncle. Fred's wife is Anna, and they married last year have a baby daughter.

Draw a family tree as stated in the passages.

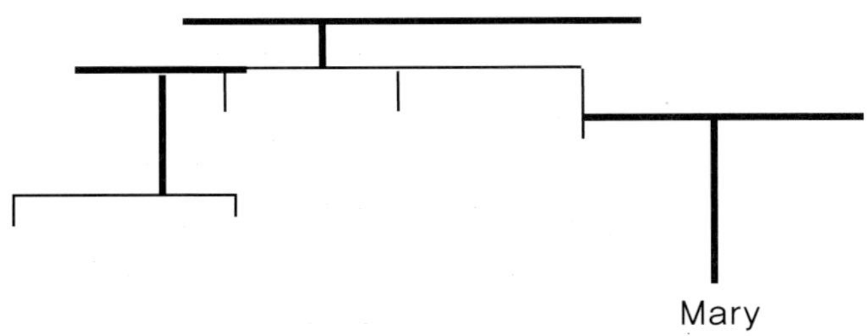

Grammar Exercises [11]

1. He wanted her _____ English writing class in this semester.
   ① to take ② taking
   ③ takes ④ take

2. I saw her _____ the piano in the hall last week.
   ① to play ② playing
   ③ plays ④ played

3. I expect him _____ the violin in the orchestra this season.
   ① to play ② playing
   ③ plays ④ paly

4. I was made _____ the test room by the supervisors.
   ① to enter ② enter
   ③ entering ④ entered

5. You had better _____ home with your friends right away.
   ① to go ② going
   ③ gone ④ go

6. He asked me _____ to the party last Saturday.

① to come ② coming

③ will come ④ come

7. I saw him _____ to church with his family on Sundays.

① to go ② going

③ gone ④ go

8. They promised the officers _____ their salary this month.

① to raise ② raising

③ raised ④ raise

9. His mother made him _____ the living room and the kitchen.

① to clean ② cleaning

③ cleaned ④ clean

10. Her mother had her daughter _____ for the party on Easter.

① to prepare ② preparing

③ prepared ④ prepare

Task Tips

Sample Questions of Date and Time

1. Date

1) What is the date today?
2) What date is it today?
3) What's today's date?
4) What day is it?
5) What month is it?
6) What year is it?
7) What's the date next Monday?
8) What was the date last Friday?
9) What day is the 17th?
10) Is the 16th a Monday or a Tuesday?
11) What month follows (comes) after May?
12) What is the day before Saturday called?

2. Time

1) What time is it?
2) What's the time?
3) What time do you make it?
4) Have you got the right time?
5) Do you have a watch?

Unit 12

Traveling and Vacation

1. Is This Seat Taken?

Kate : Excuse me. Is this seat taken?
Sam : I'm sorry. What did you say?

Kate : Oh. Will someone be using this seat?
Sam : No. You can take it.

Kate : Thanks.
Sam : Which side would you like, an aisle or a window?

Kate : I want to sit on the aisle side.
Would you mind moving to the window, please?
Sam : No, not at all.

2. I'd Like to Reserve a Room.

Grace : Good evening, sir. May I help you?

Max : Yes. I'd like to reserve a room.

Grace : Great. Do you want to stay for a vacation?

Max : Sure. What kind of room do you have?

Grace : How large is your family?

Max : Three. Two adults and one child.

Grace : Let me see. We have a room with two double beds. How long will you stay?

Max : Just two nights. We will stay two nights.

Grace : That will be three days and two nights. Right?

Max : Yes, that's right, ma'am.

3. I'm Going to Go Hiking.

Lisa : I'm so glad I finally have a long weekend.

Daniel : Me too. We've got three days in a row.
It's a long weekend.

Lisa : So, where're you going?

Daniel : I don't have any plans yet. How about you?

Lisa : I'm going to go hiking and camping in the mountains.

Daniel : That sounds exciting.

Lisa : Will you join me?

Daniel : Hm ... , let me think about it. I'll let you know later.

4. I Start to Have Summer Vacation.

Susan : Do you have school today?
Tony : My classes have finished. I start to have summer vacation.

Susan : Really? And then, what do you plan to do?
Tony : Well, I don't know yet.
What am I going to do with my free time?

Susan : Are you planning to take any summer classes?
Tony : No. I don't want to take any classes during summer.
I think I'll just relax. I really need a break.

Susan : I really envy you.

5. How Was Your Vacation?

Allen : How was your vacation, Dolly?

Dolly : Oh, it was great! I had a great time on the beach.

Allen : It sounds wonderful! You're so dark!

Dolly : Yeah. I had a lot of time on the beach.

Allen : What else did you do?

Dolly : Nothing special. It was good just to relax.

Allen : I wish I could get away like you.

Dolly : Really? I will invite you next time.

Allen : Thanks. I really envy you.

Review Exercises [Unit 12]

Read the sentence and write an appropriate answer.

1. Excuse me. Is this seat taken?

   ____

2. Will someone be using this seat?

   ____

3. Which side would you like, an aisle or an window?

   ____

4. How large is your family?

   ____

5. How long will you stay?

6. I'm so glad I finally have a long weekend.

7. Will you join me?

8. Do you have school today?

9. And then, what do you plan to do?

10. Are you planning to take any summer classes?

Storytelling (12)

Telling Numbers : Ask Questions about Your ID.

(1) What's your telephone number?
It's eight-seven-two-eight-o-nine. 872809

(2) What's your address?
Twenty-three Charles Street. 23

(3) How old are you?
Twenty-one. 21

(4) What's your passport number?
Five-six-one-three-two. 56132

(5) What's your favourite number?
Seventeen. 17

(6) What's your fax number?
Seven-o-one-six-two-four. 701624

(7) What's your student number?
two-zero-one-three-one-three-two-five. 2013-1325

Grammar Exercises [12]

1. On _____ at the station, she immediately took a taxi.

① arrive ② arrived

③ arriving ④ to arrive

2. He feels like _____ a trip with family this summer.

① take ② took

③ taking ④ to take

3. She visited her husband's office without _____ to him.

① notice ② noticed

③ noticing ④ to notice

4. He makes a point of _____ out after finishing homework.

① eat ② ate

③ eating ④ to eat

5. Would you mind _____ me the way to the library?

① tell ② told

③ telling ④ to tell

6. They will ask some questions after they finish _____ the text.

① read ② reads

③ reading ④ to read

7. The heavy snow prevented them from _____ to school for days.

① go ② went

③ going ④ to go

8. Mrs. Ellis is always proud of her son's _____ a soldier.

① be ② was

③ being ④ to be

9. Mr. Ferguson is sure of her daughter's _____ the exam.

① pass ② passed

③ passing ④ to pass

10. The baby is always afraid of _____ alone at night.

① sleep ② slept

③ sleeping ④ to sleep

Task Tips

Sample Questions of Weather and Identity

1. Weather

   1) What is the weather like?
   2) Is it cold or hot?
   3) What is the forecast for next week?
   4) What temperature is it?
   5) Is it below freezing?
   6) How many degrees below is it?
   7) What season is it?
   8) Is it raining (snowing, sleeting, hailing, winding)?

2. Identity

   1) Who are you?
   2) What is your name?
   3) How do you spell it?
   4) What is your English name?
   5) Where do you live?
   6) What is your address?
   7) Which part are you from?
   8) Where are you from?
   9) Where do you come from?
   10) Whereabouts in Seoul do you live?
   11) How old are you?
   12) Which school do you go to?
   13) Who is your English teacher?

Unit 13

Job Interview

1. What about Your Work Experience?

Interviewer : Good afternoon. Please, have a seat.
Interviewee : Thank you.

Interviewer : Well, could you tell me a little about your background?
Interviewee : Yes, I graduated from Kookje College in 2012.
My major was tourism management.

Interviewer : I see. Now what about your work experience?
Interviewee : After graduation, I worked as a reporter for the Seoul News.

Interviewer : How was it at the Seoul News?
Interviewee : Well, I liked it a lot. The people and my boss were great.
They were understanding and helpful.

Interviewer : Why did you apply here?

Interviewee : I think this company is better for my future plan.

Interviewer : Well, thank you for your application.
We'll make a decision and call you in a couple of days.

Interviewee : Thank you for seeing me. I hope to see you again.

2. I'm Calling for a Job Application.

Mrs. Russell : Hello.

Jim : Hi. This is Jim Kim.
I'm calling for the job opening you advertised.

Mrs. Russell : Yes. We're looking for a secretary who speak English.

Jim : What should I do to apply?

Mrs. Russell : You can send your resume by e-mail, first.
And we will contact you for an interview.

Jim : All right. I'll do them first.
Thanks for your help. Bye.

3. How Do I Apply for the Position?

Julian : What are you going to do after you graduate?

Patrick : Well, I'm preparing for the national civil service exam.
I'd like to work for a social welfare.
How about you?

Julian : I'm going to apply to several tourist agencies.
I want to get the position of tourist information manager.

Patrick : I think you studied a lot about that position.

Julian : Right. But how do I apply for the position?

Patrick : You can go to the career placement officers at the department.
The counselors at school will help you.

Julian : Thank you for the information. Good luck in the future.

4. I Have to Prepare for the Interview.

Molly : I just got a call from the office I applied to last week.
I'm scheduled for an interview tomorrow.

Andy : Great. Congratulations!

Molly : Thanks. I've got to do well at the interview.
Do you have any tips?

Andy : First, you have to put on the right kind of clothes.

Molly : I'm going to wear a conservative outfit.

Andy : Second, you should make a list of some answers about you.
They will ask some important questions. Right?

Molly : Okay. I have to prepare for some answers on the interview.

Review Exercises [Unit 13]

Read the sentence and write an appropriate answer.

1. Could you tell me a little about your background?

____

2. Now what about your work experience?

____

3. Why did you apply here?

____

4. I'm calling for the job opening you advertised.

____

5. What should I do to apply?

____

6. What are you going to do after you graduate?

____

7. I'd like to work for a social welfare. How about you?

____

8. How do I apply for the position?

____

9. Do you have any tips?

____

10. They will ask some important questions. Right?

____

Storytelling [13]

Classroom Display

Our classroom is very comfortable. There is a picture on the wall near the door. In front of the picture, there is a desk and a chair for a professor. There are some books on the desk. In front of the classroom, there is a big board. At the back of the classroom, there is a board. At the side of the classroom, there is a window. Above the window, there are some shelves. Next to the shelves is a map of the world. There are 25 desks and chairs in the center of the classroom. There are six lights on the ceiling and a large door in front of the classroom.

Choose a room and describe it to your friend.

Grammar Exercises [13]

1. The workers met _____ management to discuss the new contract.

   ① at ② for
   ③ with ④ under

2. The company is located _____ the street.

   ① across ② in
   ③ next ④ over

3. I work _____ the sales department at the department store.

   ① at ② by
   ③ for ④ in

4. The producer accepted the award _____ of his talented musician.

   ① on behalf ② half
   ③ by means ④ for

5. It is necessary to deliver orders _____ time.

   ① at ② on
   ③ due ④ with

6. The country is famous _____ its diamond mines.

① for ② as

③ by ④ with

7. This package will arrive at least _____ noon next week.

① on ② for

③ at ④ in

8. We hope to arrange a joint venture _____ a company in Seoul.

① on ② in

③ at ④ with

9. Mary has been married _____ Jimmy for two years.

① on ② to

③ at ④ by

10. Most of the guest speakers arrived _____ plane.

① on ② to

③ from ④ by

Task Tips

Country and the Capital City

	Country (나라)	Capital City (수도)
1	Austria	Vienna
2	Denmark	Copenhagen
3	England	London
4	Finland	Helsinki
5	France	Paris
6	Germany	Berlin
7	Greece	Athens
8	Ireland	Dublin
9	Italy	Rome
10	Russian Federation	Moscow
11	Spain	Madrid
12	Egypt	Cairo
13	Kenya	Nairobi
14	China	Beijing
15	India	New Delhi

저 · 자 · 약 · 력

정은주(Eun Joo Jeong)
영문학박사(세종대학교 대학원 영어영문학과, 영미문학전공)
현) 국제대학교 관광경영계열 부교수

고인숙(Inn Sook Koh)
영문학박사(성균관대학교 대학원 영어영문학과, 영미문학전공)
현) 국제대학교 관광경영계열 부교수

김상원(Sang Won Kim)
이화여자대학교 영어교육학과 박사과정
현) 국제대학교 호텔외식조리과 조교수

심재황(Jaehwang Shim)
영어학박사(중앙대학교 대학원 응용언어학)
중앙대 강사, 국제대 강사
가천대 교육대학원, 일반대학원 외래교수
아세아연합신학대 선교대학원 외래교수

New Practical English (I)

2013년 3월 2일 초판 1쇄 인쇄
2013년 3월 5일 초판 1쇄 발행

저 자 정은주•고인숙•김상원•심재황
펴낸이 임순재
펴낸곳 한올출판사
등록 제11-403호
121-849
주 소 서울시 마포구 성산동 133-3 한올빌딩 3층
전 화 (02)376-4298(대표)
팩 스 (02)302-8073
홈페이지 www.hanol.co.kr
e-메일 hanol@hanol.co.kr
정 가 15,000원 (CD포함)

• ISBN 978-89-98636-08-1